REMOTE TEAM INTERACTIONS WORKBOOK

USING TEAM TOPOLOGIES PATTERNS
FOR REMOTE WORKING

REMOTE TEAM INTERACTIONS WORKBOOK

MATTHEW SKELTON AND MANUEL PAIS

IT Revolution
Portland, Oregon

25 NW 23rd Pl, Suite 6314
Portland, OR 97210

First Edition
Printed in the United States of America

27 26 25 24 23 22   1 2 3 4 5 6 7 8 9 10

Cover and book design by Devon Smith

ISBN: 9781950508617
eBook ISBN: 9781950508624
Web PDF ISBN: 9781950508631

For information about special discounts for bulk purchases, or for information
on booking authors for an event, please visit our website at ITRevolution.com.

REMOTE TEAM INTERACTIONS WORKBOOK

CONTENTS

Preface   vii

Introduction   ix

   A Brief Overview of Team Topologies   ix

   How to Use This Workbook   x

Chapter 1 Overview: Focus on Remote Team Interactions   **1**

   What Does an Organization Need in Order to Thrive in
a Remote-First World?   1

     Resource: Cognitive Load Assessment   3

   Use the Team API Approach to Define and Communicate
Responsibilities and Team Focus   4

   Track Dependencies Using Simple Tools and Remove
Blocking Dependencies   4

   Overcommunicate Using Just Enough Written
Documentation   5

   Summary: Design and Define the Ways in Which
Teams Interact   6

Chapter 2 Team Dependencies   **7**

   Team API   7

     Resource: Team API Exercise   11

   Tracking Dependencies   14

     Resource: Team Dependencies Tracking Exercise   17

   Building Networks: Coffee, Talks, Internal Conferences   18

Chapter 3 Setting Team Boundaries   **23**

   Group Trust Boundaries   23

     Resource: Trust Boundaries Exercise   26

   Online Space Setup   27

Resource: Online Space Assessment   *32*

Team-Focused Conventions for Chat Tools   34

Chapter 4   Purposeful Interactions   **37**

Team Interaction Modes: A Review   37

Listening to Team Interactions   43

Clarity Communication Purpose and Channels   47

Ensuring Clarity of Purpose of Platforms and Services   49

Resource: Example Wiki Page: Thinnest Viable

Platform Template   *53*

Chapter 5   Next Steps   **55**

Design and Conduct a Developer Experience

Platform Survey   55

Define Naming and Usage Conventions for Chat

Tools   57

Use the Team API with Multiple Teams to Define and

Clarify Team Boundaries   58

Devise and Share an Execution Plan   58

List of Resources   61

Notes   63

About the Authors   67

About *Team Topologies*   68

PREFACE

Why We Wrote This Workbook

The COVID-19 pandemic of 2020 and beyond has ushered in a new remote-first world for IT along with most other departments in the business. But many organizations have struggled to catch up with new tooling and ways of working. While some companies have embraced this new reality—ditching their expensive downtown offices and telling staff they can work from home permanently—many more organizations are discovering for the first time that the physical office was covering up poorly defined teams and poorly defined areas of focus, threatening their DevOps transformation efforts and the overall health and success of their business.

A successful remote-first approach requires the explicit design of communication between teams using physical and online spaces. Using simple tools for dependency tracking and patterns from *Team Topologies*, such as the team API, organizations will find that well-defined team interactions are key to effective IT delivery in the remote-first world.

In this workbook, we explore several aspects of team-first remote work, including:

- how the new "remote-first" world is highlighting existing poor team interactions within organizations
- why organizations should use the team API pattern to define and communicate the focus of teams
- how organizations can track and remove team-level dependencies
- how and why organizations should design inter-team communications consciously
- why and how organizations can use the three team interaction modes from *Team Topologies* (collaboration, X-as-a-Service, and facilitating) to help.

We hope these ideas and patterns will help you and your organization become more effective with a team-based, remote-first approach to building and running software systems.

Also, we'd like to thank Rich Allen for his invaluable contributions to this workbook.

—Matthew Skelton and Manuel Pais
August 2021

INTRODUCTION

A Brief Overview of Team Topologies

Team Topologies is the leading approach to organizing business and technology teams for fast flow, providing a practical, step-by-step, adaptive model for organizational design and team interaction. The Team Topologies ecosystem of partners, practitioners, and learning academy is transforming the approach to the digital operating model for organizations around the world.

In the Team Topologies model, four fundamental types of teams and three core team interaction modes combine with awareness of Conway's Law, team cognitive load, and responsive organization evolution to define a no-nonsense, team-friendly, humanistic approach to building and running software systems.

The four fundamental types of teams are:

- **Stream-aligned team:** aligned to a flow of work from (usually) a segment of the business domain.
- **Enabling team:** helps a stream-aligned team to overcome obstacles. Also detects missing capabilities.
- **Complicated-subsystem team:** where significant mathematics, calculations, and technical expertise is needed.
- **Platform team:** a grouping of other team types that provide a compelling internal product to accelerate delivery by stream-aligned teams.

READ MORE

You can read more about the four fundamental types of teams in *Team Topologies* on pages 79–110.

There are three ways in which teams should interact (interaction modes):

- **Collaboration:** working together for a defined period of time to discover new things (APIs, practices, technologies, etc.).
- **X-as-a-Service:** one team provides and one team consumes something "as a service."
- **Facilitating:** one team helps and mentors another team.

> **READ MORE**
>
> You can read more about the three interaction modes in *Team Topologies* on pages 131–152.

The basic principles behind *Team Topologies* help organizations take a team-first approach to help unblock flow.

> **RESOURCE**
>
> You can also download the "Team Topologies in a Nutshell" and "Getting Started with Team Topologies" infographics at TeamTopologies.com.

How to Use this Workbook

We begin this workbook with an overview of the mindset and skills you and your organization will need to succeed in a remote-first world. The three main chapters (2, 3, and 4) each feature three patterns for improving team-based work in a remote-first context. Each improvement pattern has some explanatory context along with an example and suggestions for how to try it in your organization (labeled *Now Your Turn*). Each improvement pattern also refers to a section of the original *Team Topologies* book to provide a more detailed explanation, like this:

> **READ MORE**
>
> Read more about setting up team-first physical and online/virtual spaces in *Team Topologies*, pages 50–55.

While it's not necessary to read *Team Topologies* to take advantage of the patterns in this workbook, for the best results we recommend that you take time to contextualize the patterns of this workbook in combination with the ideas in the *Team Topologies* book.

Many of the patterns in this workbook also reference templates and other resources. Where possible, we've recreated the templates and resources for you in this workbook. We also provide links to these templates and resources online, so you can use them to get started. These online resources are free to use and open to contributions and suggestions for improvements. These tips will be featured like this:

> **RESOURCE**
>
> Use the Trust Boundaries template at GitHub.com/TeamTopologies/Trust-Boundaries-Template.

We've also worked to show the various ideas or techniques in the workbook that are related so that it is easy for you to navigate and make connections. These relationships are shown like this:

> Chapter 2 in this workbook has more details on team APIs.

We hope these callouts help you navigate and get the most out of this workbook.

CHAPTER 1

Overview—Focus on Remote Team Interactions

Aremote-first way of working requires a new mindset from organizations. This overview chapter explores some of the techniques that can help organizations adopt an effective remote-first approach.

What Does an Organization Need in Order to Thrive in a Remote-First World?

Many organizations have found, to their dismay, that rolling out a new chat tool for staff working remotely does not magically make the organization remote-first. A viable remote-first approach needs more than just chat and video tools.

Certainly, tools are needed and useful, but for a successful digital transformation—whether colocated or remote-first—the organization also needs good psychological safety and an effective set of "ground rules" and practices for teams to use for working together.

An example of this is Google's five keys to successful teams. As they lay out, "Who is on a team matters less than how the team members interact, structure their work, and view their contributions."[1]

They describe these five key dynamics as:[2]

1. **Psychological safety**: Can teams take risks without feeling insecure?
2. **Dependability**: Can teams count on one another?
3. **Structure and clarity**: Are there clear goals, roles, and execution plans?
4. **Meaning of work**: Is the work personally important to the team?
5. **Impact of work**: Does the team believe the work matters?

Clear ground rules and practices define ways of working, set expectations, and provide easy-to-recognize patterns and modes of behavior that make it easy for people to work in well-defined ways. In particular, well-defined team interactions clarify the relationships between different groups in the organization and the purpose of different activities. This in turn helps to minimize the cognitive load on teams and provides more "head space" for focusing on the most important aspects of work within the organization.

Broadly speaking, cognitive load is the amount of mental effort being used on a task or set of tasks. For teams, you can think of cognitive load as the collective amount of mental effort being used by the team.

READ MORE

You can read more on cognitive load as it pertains to teams in *Team Topologies*, pages 11–12 and 39–47.

Cognitive Load Assessment

You can use this survey template as a starting point to assess the overall cognitive load of your team.

Answer each question on a scale of 1 (very poor) to 5 (very good).

1. How is the experience of building your services? Things to consider: Is building a clear and repeatable task? Is it fast "enough"? What happens when builds fail? Are failures easy to diagnose?
2. How is the experience of testing your services? Things to consider: Is testing a clear and repeatable task? Is it fast "enough"? What happens when tests fail? Are failures easy to diagnose? Are test environments adequate? Are test environments easy to access/ spin up/clean up/inject test data into?
3. How is the experience of deploying your services? Things to consider: Are deployments a clear and repeatable task? Do you know what the deployment strategy is? What happens when deployments fail? Is it possible and straightforward to roll back a failed deployment? Do you have access to the necessary logs to understand why a deployment failed and/or its current status?

4. How is the experience of operating your services? Things to consider: Do you know how each service is being monitored? Do you have access to the data? Are adequate alerts (few false positives) being sent? Are logs and information accessible and easy to find? Are data flows across services relatively easy to follow?

5. How is the experience of being on call for your services? Things to consider: Do you know what the incident response procedure is? Do you feel you have enough experience (either real or simulated) to deal with incidents without high levels of stress? Do you know who to reach out to for help during an incident when you're on call? Would you be anxious about a 3 a.m. outage? What about an incident in a service that hasn't been modified for months or years?

6. How is the experience of dealing with health industry regulations and compliance? Things to consider: Do you feel you have sufficient awareness to raise questions on changes that might require compliance oversight or at least a quick debrief? Are you confident that you know which industry regulations are of concern for your services? If yes, do you feel that this knowledge is being refreshed often enough?

7. Would you like to comment on your overall engineering experience?

Notice that questions #1 through #5 focus on the experience of building, testing, deploying, and supporting software services, so they are broadly applicable. However, question #6 is specific to an organization working in the healthcare industry. It is included as an example of the kind of context-specific questions you will need to use in order to assess other aspects that might be causing high cognitive load for your teams.

The point is that this form is just a starting point. You will need to adapt and expand it to your organization's specific needs.

RESOURCE

You can access an online form of this assessment here: GitHub.com/TeamTopologies/Team-Cognitive-Load-Assessment.

Use the Team API Approach to Define and Communicate Responsibilities and Team Focus

So what approaches can organizations take to improve interactions between teams? In *Team Topologies*, we explain the concept of a team API. A regular API is an application programming interface, a technical term for the way one piece of software interacts with another piece of software programmatically. A given team's API is therefore a kind of specification for how other teams in the organization can and should interact with that team.

> **READ MORE**
>
> Read more on team APIs in *Team Topologies*, pages 47–49.

The team API covers a wide range of aspects, including:

- artifacts owned by the team (libraries, applications, services, etc.)
- versioning and testing approaches
- wikis and documentation
- practices and principles
- road map and priorities
- communication preferences (when/how)

By defining these aspects and making them easily discoverable by other teams, a team increases its clarity of purpose and helps other groups to understand how that team fits into the wider organization.

> See Chapter 2 of this workbook for more on team APIs, including exercises/templates.

Track Dependencies Using Simple Tools and Remove Blocking Dependencies

All teams are part of a socio-technical system, and therefore depend on other teams at some point in time, to a greater or lesser extent. That means we should be tracking dependencies between teams now and over time. Some dependencies might be fine today, but in a few months from now they will start slowing down the dependent team too much and we'll need to address it.

While ideally we might want to remove all dependencies, in practice we should identify which ones are problematic and should be removed, and which ones are "under control," for now at least. A problematic dependency introduces significant delays, is too unpredictable, or increases work in progress (WIP) for the dependent team, slowing them down considerably.

A remote-first environment creates unique challenges in this space. It's impossible to simply walk up to the desk of someone on another team to ask about progress. But a constant stream of chat messages asking for status updates becomes a cognitive burden.

Instead of spending time waiting on other teams to finish their work, focus on tracking and then removing these in-flow dependencies. Books like *Making Work Visible* by Dominica DeGrandis explain useful techniques for visualizing team dependencies, many of which can easily be adapted to work in a fully remote context. DeGrandis also has a great article on *TechBeacon*, "How to Defrag Your DevOps Value Stream," that can be useful.[3]

> Chapter 2 of this workbook has more details and exercises on tracking and removing in-flow dependencies.

Overcommunicate Using Just Enough Written Documentation

In a remote work setting, it's vital to "overcommunicate." As Meaghan Lewis outlines in her article on *TechBeacon*, communicating mainly through text messages or chats makes discerning tone and urgency challenging, not to mention problems arising from cultural differences in phrases. Also, navigating when and how to post (to an individual or the whole team) is new territory.[4]

Ultimately, in a remote-work world it is essential to be very clear all the time about *what* you are working on, *why* you're working on it, *how* your work is being completed, and *when* it should be completed by. Overcommunication feels almost like an externalization of your key decisions and reasoning so that people can easily reconstruct the sequence of thoughts that led you to your current work. It is vital to successful remote teams.

Overcommunication will take several forms: share small decisions in a chat tool, write up larger decisions or designs in a wiki or document, and even create a presentation or report to explain important concepts. Don't just rely on people seeing scrolling messages in the chat tool.

Because most human-to-human interaction in a remote-first organization or team will be via chat and text media (such as wikis, documents, and so on), it is essential to emphasize good written skills. It's not just about typing lots of text, though. The text needs to have context when seen by itself.

For example, chatting "Hi, what do you think?" requires a mental context-switch for the person reading the message. What does that question refer to? They might even have to scroll back through a series of chats to find the original ask. On the other hand, "Hi. So, do you think we should switch component A for component B due to the performance issues with A?" gives plenty of context for the reader. There's no need for them to hunt down the original question or chat thread.

Don't make it hard for people to discover meaning in written communications. Make the messages self-contained.

Summary: Design and Define the Ways in Which Teams Interact

Well-defined interactions are key to effective teams, and this is especially true for remote work situations. Team-focused conventions within chat tools and wiki documentation increase discoverability and reduce cognitive load on communications. For example, using a chat tool like Slack you can enforce predictable channel naming conventions. Plus, the chat tool's ability to search across channels increases discoverability.

By adopting clear ground rules and practices, like the team API and predictable chat tool naming conventions (discussed in Chapter 3), organizations can take advantage of remote-first ways of working to increase their chances of success.

CHAPTER 2

Team Dependencies

Dependencies between teams are a reality in any organization, even when we try to minimize them. If we don't track team dependencies in the first place, we will run into scheduling and prioritization problems that slow down the flow of delivery. To understand inter-team dependencies, the work being done by each team needs to be visible. Once we are able to track these dependencies, we can then look into promoting healthy dependencies and removing (or minimizing the impact of) slowing or blocking dependencies. This chapter explores techniques to track and manage inter-team dependencies that work in a remote context.

Team API

The first step to start identifying team dependencies is for each team to clarify and provide visibility to the whole organization on the work they are currently doing and their priorities for the (near) future. Rather than starting with a top-down view of all the work in progress across the organization, we should promote that each team surfaces and exposes that information to others in all directions (upward, sideways, and downward) in an easy-to-consume way.

This decentralized approach also supports the fact that different teams might prefer to work with different timescales. For instance, some teams might only plan the current two-week sprint and prioritize high-level work items for the next couple of sprints, while other teams might do detailed monthly or quarterly plans. Teams also work with different artifacts—Scrum or Kanban boards or planning documents—depending on the team's approach to work and, sometimes, the nature of the services they are delivering.

In Chapter 3 of *Team Topologies* we introduced the idea of a team API, a clear interface describing different aspects related to team ownership, communication preferences, practices, and principles. For example: Which artifacts does the team own? Which practices do they use to develop, test, version, and deliver those artifacts? Etc.

In the context of remote teams, it is even more important to include in the team API the road map for upcoming work as well as communication preferences, such as which channels (e.g., chat tools, video conferencing, email, or phone) they use, which days of the week and times are more suitable, and what the expected response time on asynchronous channels should be.

Making access to information and the team as clear as possible minimizes the cognitive load on others. It allows people to quickly find out who they need to talk to for a specific question, as well as when and how to talk to a specific team when it is needed. Even in situations where the team API does not provide all the necessary details, it should at least clarify when and how best to reach the team with further questions.

In addition to communicating preferences to other teams, the use of team APIs encourages a team to deliberately consider how they want to be viewed by and how they want to interact with people outside of the team. Teams can begin to define their own API independently from each other. This can lead to increased clarity and more purposeful communications and interactions between teams, provided they follow a consistent format that is easy to consume by people outside of the team.

> **READ MORE**
>
> Read more about team APIs in *Team Topologies,* pages 47–49.

Example

In the first half of 2020, Zoom and other video communication tools saw exponential growth due to worldwide lockdowns caused by the COVID-19 pandemic. This unexpected growth put a great strain on these companies' infrastructure and security. It's not hard to imagine an identity management team in this situation buried with change requests to natively support more runtime platforms as well as fix security issues getting media attention. Let's look at a fictitious company, Mooz, and their fictitious identity management team.

The use of a team API for the Mooz identity management team is even more critical in this situation, as the team attempts to navigate the storm of work befallen upon them. When a team like this is under pressure to deliver on their goals, the use of a well-known, easy-to-access team API could help other teams and individuals in the organization communicate their needs or issues in a way that is efficient for this team, reducing interruptions and their need to context switch. This will allow the identity management team to focus on the work at hand. There may be a need for other teams to collaborate with them for a short period in order to configure their authentication workflow.

The team API can also be used to define how the team prefers to use chat communication tools, such as Slack. (In fact, at the company Slack, instructions for how to request help from a team are often pinned to the channel.)[1] For more complicated situations, a workflow builder can be used to ensure all requests are asked in a consistent, pro-forma enforced structure. The team should also look to be more purposeful about how those Slack channels are organized where possible.

> Chapter 3 of this workbook has more details on creating team conventions for chat tools.

The following team API example is from the imaginary Mooz identity management team.

Team Identity Management API

Updated: 2nd June 2021

Team name and focus: Team Identity Management is responsible for the identity management service
Team type: Platform team
Part of a platform? Yes, the Engineering Foundations platform
Do we provide a service to other teams? Yes
- Details: An identity management service allowing users to authenticate and access resources provided by other teams

What "service level expectations" do other teams have of us?
- Support requests to be acknowledged within 1 hour of submission
- First response to support requests within 24 hours of submission

Software owned and evolved by this team: Github: mooz_inc/
identity.management
Versioning approaches: Semantic versioning on nuget packages
Wiki search terms: Identity, access, ActiveDirectory
Chat tool channels:
- #platformteam-identitymgmt
- #support-identitymgmt
- #releases-identitymgmt

Time of daily sync meeting:
- 9 a.m., accessible via https://mooz.us/k/7846891894 (non-team members are welcome to join but please mute yourself until the questions section at the end of the call)

What we're currently working on:
- **our services and systems:** an identity client allowing other teams to more easily integrate with the identity management system
- **ways of working:** adopting daily showcases for a 2-week period, accessible via https://mooz.us/k/7846891894 (everyone is welcome to join but please mute yourself and use the "raise hand" feature to ask a question during the showcase)
- **wider cross-team or organizational improvements:** helping to bootstrap the new internal tech conference

Teams we currently interact with:

Team Name	Interaction Mode	Purpose	Duration
Test Automation Enabling Team	Facilitating	Understand test automation and data mgmt examples for iOS	2 months (from Mar 30 to May 29, 1 day per week)
VideoCalls Stream Team	Collaboration	Define workflow for authentication errors in VideoCalls service	3 weeks (from Apr 13 to Apr 30, 2h per day)

Teams we expect to interact with soon:

Team Name	Interaction Mode	Purpose	Duration
CallAdmin Stream Team	Collaboration	Clarify and test authentication permissions for new CallAdmin standalone app	2 weeks (from May 1 to May 14, 2h per day)

Now Your Turn

Think about a team within your current organization. What might their team API look like? Put together a team API that provides members of your organization who are outside of that team a clear description of the team's purpose, their ways of working, and how they interact with other teams. Next, think about where you might want to store the team API to make it easily accessible to other members of your organization.

Team API Exercise

Use this template to help your team(s) think about their team API. Each team should answer the questions and fill in the details below. Remember that the answers and details will be a point-in-time snapshot of team relationships and team interactions.

About Team [TEAM NAME HERE]

Date:_____

Team name and focus:_____

Team type:_____

Part of a Platform? (Y/N)

Details:_____

Do we provide a service to other teams? (Y/N)

Details:_____

What kind of service level expectations (SLE) do other teams have of us? _____

Software owned and evolved by this team:_____

Versioning approaches: _____

Wiki search terms:_____

Chat tool channels:

- # _____

- # _____

Time of daily sync meeting: _____

Team type: (stream-aligned, enabling, complicated subsystem, platform) _____

What we're currently working on:

- Our services and systems: _____

- Ways of working: _____

- Wider cross-team or organizational improvements:_____

Teams we currently interact with:

Team name/ Focus	Interaction Mode*	Purpose	Duration

*Team interaction modes: (collaboration, X-as-a-Service, facilitating)

Teams we expect to interact with soon:

Team name/ Focus	Interaction Mode*	Purpose	Duration

*Team interaction modes: (collaboration, X-as-a-Service, facilitating)

RESOURCE

You can download a blank template of the team API to use with your teams here: GitHub.com/TeamTopologies/Team-API-Template.

As you work on your team APIs, make sure you categorize each team as one of the fundamental team types (stream-aligned, platform, enabling, or complicated subsystem). Then detail how you would expect other teams to communicate with them using chat tools, etc.

Also consider the following:

- What about the team's current road map?
- What are they currently working on and what are they planning to work on in the near future that may affect other teams in your organization?
- Who would need to know about that and how could they best be notified?
- Perhaps a specific chat tool channel could be used, allowing those interested to follow the channel and keep up to date with the latest news.

READ MORE

The four fundamental team types are discussed on pages 79–110 of *Team Topologies*.

Tracking Dependencies

Since all teams are part of a wider socio-technical system, it is inevitable that teams will depend on each other at some point in time. When applying the principles of Team Topologies, one of the goals is to reduce dependencies between teams by increasing or giving full ownership of end-to-end systems or services to individual teams. However, completely eradicating all dependencies is hardly ever 100% achievable. It is important to recognize this.

It is also important to recognize that there are different types of dependencies. There are blocking dependencies (they stop the flow of work, introducing wait times) versus non-blocking, healthy versus unhealthy, frequent versus infrequent, and more. Since dependencies can never be fully eradicated, it is important to track dependencies between teams and their type now and over time.

For example, something that starts as a blocking dependency could evolve into a non-blocking dependency. This is a good thing, as it should result in increased autonomy for the dependent team. Unfortunately, it is equally possible for healthy dependencies to transition into unhealthy ones, which can begin to slow down a dependent team too much.

In practice, we should look to record the dependencies that a team has and identify which ones are "under control" (for the time being, at least) and which ones are problematic and need to be addressed or even removed. Problematic dependencies can result in significant delays, introduce unpredictability, and increase the amount of work in progress (WIP) for the dependent team.

When tracking dependencies, the important thing to note is not the documentation in and of itself but rather that the tracker can be used to assess how dependencies should change. Are we okay with a blocking dependency on this other team? What could we change to avoid a blocking dependency? Is it possible to collaborate with the other team for a period of time to make the dependency non-blocking or at least less frequent?

By making the dependencies visible, each team is able to visualize their different dependencies, allowing them to work on reducing the ones that are negatively affecting the flow of work.

Of course, there are different ways to track dependencies between teams, such as with dependency boards or dependency tags as exemplified in *Making Work Visible* by Dominica DeGrandis.

One of DeGrandis's examples is the Physical Dependency Matrix (featured on the next page). This matrix helps teams organize and visualize dependencies, and could be easily recreated using an online tool for remote teams.

INCOMING DEPENDENCIES ↓ / OUTGOING DEPENDENCIES →	Form button	tabbed panel	Param	Remote call UI	Component-fly	Restful action	Action Mapper	Filter dispatcher	Servlet dispatcher	Portlet url Helper
Form button										
tabbed panel	1									
Param	3	7								
Remote Call UI	6				8	2	6	9		
Component-fly		5	7				11	10		
Restful Action		3								
Action mapper		2								
filter dispatcher				10					4	
Servlet dispatcher		5								
Portlet Url Helper						2				

Numbers in the boxes refer to the number of times that the dependency occurs, from the component shown at the top to the component shown on the left.

Physical Dependency Matrix

Source: Dominica DeGrandis, *Making Work Visible: Exposing Time Theft to Optimize Work & Flow* (Portland, OR: IT Revolution, 2017), 79.

She also shows how teams can use simple kanban boards to visualize dependencies (two examples are provided below). With multiple tools available for online kanbans, this can be a great option for remote teams.

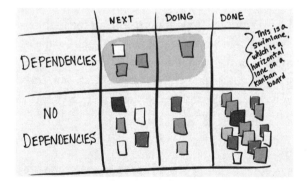

This is a swimlane, which is a horizontal lane on a kanban board

Dependency Swimlane Board

Source: Dominica DeGrandis, *Making Work Visible: Exposing Time Theft to Optimize Work & Flow* (Portland, OR: IT Revolution, 2017), 81.

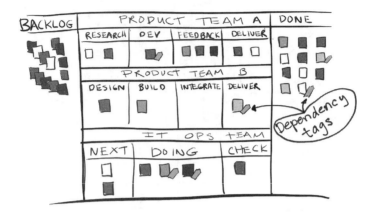

Dependency Tags on Kanban Cards

Source: Dominica DeGrandis, *Making Work Visible: Exposing Time Theft to Optimize Work & Flow* (Portland, OR: IT Revolution, 2017), 81.

Many of the examples in *Making Work Visible* can be easily adjusted for remote-first teams using tools such as Mural, Miro, Trello, and more.

READ MORE

Read more about dependencies between teams in *Team Topologies* on pages 74–75.

Example: Dependency Tracker for Teams

Below is an example team dependency tracker. In this example, a team is working on content for a music streaming service. Their work also requires that they interact with many other teams across the value stream, such as Operations, Storage, Recommendations, and Data Admin.

RESOURCE

Download a blank team dependencies tracker to use with your teams here: GitHub.com/TeamTopologies/Team-Dependencies-Tracking.

Team name/ focus	Depends on team	Type (blocking/ slowing/ok)	Short description of dependency (artifacts, approvals, other)
Music Content	Ops	Slowing	Need machines, connections, help to set up things. Generally works well, but at times the workload on Ops causes the lead times to grow and slow us down.
Music Content	Storage	No problem	Storage. Not big, mostly information/ communication needs to happen.
Music Content	Recommendations	No problem	Recommendations service integration when there's a new type of content.
Music Content	Data Admin	Blocking	Waiting for necessary data dumps for our analytics.

Now Your Turn

Using the above example as a starting point, think about some of the teams within your organization. How do they currently interact? What are the dependencies between them? Are they slowing or blocking another team from getting work done? What is the reason for the dependency?

Populate a team dependency tracker for each of the teams so you have a clear record that can be used to monitor those dependencies over time.

Team Dependencies Tracking Exercise

In the famous "Spotify Model," Spotify tracked dependencies between teams over time with a simple spreadsheet. They would ask all their squads which other squads they depended on and to what extent those dependencies were blocking or slowing them down.

They would then address the blocking and cross-tribe dependencies (namely through reorganization, architectural changes, or technical solutions), while continuing to monitor the remaining ones.[2] This same method can be used to track team dependencies at any organization.

Based on work from Spotify, this team dependencies tracker template helps teams to frame conversations around improving flow, avoiding blocking waits, and ultimately moving to a more autonomous delivery model.

Team name/ focus	Depends on Team	Type (blocking/ slowing/ok)	Short description of dependency (artifacts, approvals, other)

Building Networks: Coffee, Talks, Internal Conferences

Anyone familiar with working in an office environment has probably experienced informal social networks. These tend to occur within the office during the working day, such as when you go to the coffee machine and meet someone or when you chat with someone at lunchtime or by the water cooler.

In the physical world, you may have had lunchtime talks or maybe departmental or whole company conferences, all of which were aimed at sharing knowledge and keeping people interacting with one another, making social contact. In remote settings, it is important to keep those types of interactions running. The format will need to be different and you may need to work harder to include people, but don't just drop them because you are no longer in the same building.

A 2021 study of 61,182 Microsoft employees' interactions over the first six months of 2020 (when the COVID-19 pandemic caused lockdowns in many parts of the world) showed that Microsoft's "firm-wide remote work caused the collaboration network of workers to become more static and siloed, with fewer bridges between disparate parts."[3] As a consequence, it was "harder for employees to acquire and share new information across the network."[4]

To counter the tendency for isolation when working remotely, teams in some companies have deliberately created a fifteen- or twenty-minute virtual coffee break. Participants each agree to grab a coffee or their drink of choice and then join a virtual video call to talk about random stuff that has nothing to do with work. David Heath, lead developer at the UK's Government Digital Service, mentioned in a tweet that they experimented with "speed networking" sessions (three five-minute pairwise conversations using video breakout rooms) across the organization.[5]

These types of activities can be very valuable. They help foster informal networks of people who will be able to rely on each other down the line. They help form trust between the participants. And they help create an awareness of what else is happening outside of the confines of any individual team. During a facilitating phase (one of the three interaction modes of Team Topologies) between teams, enabling teams are able to provide targeted, on-the-ground knowledge that product or stream-aligned teams need.

However, there are opportunities for the wider sharing of knowledge by using communities of practice (CoP) or guilds to help increase awareness and capabilities within other teams. A CoP provides more widespread knowledge sharing that can help foster a sharing culture and a feeling of belonging for people with similar interests.

In her book *Building Successful Communities of Practice*, Emily Webber says "Communities of practice create the right environment for social learning, experiential learning, and a rounded curriculum, leading to accelerated learning for members."[6] It is therefore very important in the remote world that you maintain these types of meetings and encourage attendance and interaction on a regular basis, such as weekly or monthly.

One final option within larger organizations is the use of internal conferences. These can make a significant impact on an organization's level of sharing, learning, and communication by accelerating multi-team learning across departments. The need for these kinds of events is greater than ever before in a remote-first world. Being able to put on a good internal conference has always been crucial, but it is important to recognize that how you run these events will need to be adapted for the remote world.

RESOURCE

The book *Internal Tech Conferences* by Victoria Morgan-Smith and Matthew Skelton has a wealth of advice on running internal conferences. For example, you will need to consider how you achieve interaction between the speaker and attendees, and whether to use prerecorded talks to help avoid the need for expensive broadcast technology. It may be necessary to train and mentor speakers on how to give online talks. Your speakers may even require new equipment to avoid poor audio or video, which can distract or even impede the ability of your audience to fully engage with the content.

It is also important to note that live-streaming talks can exclude people in regions with limited bandwidth, or create conflicts with organizations who have staff across multiple time zones. Visit InternalTechConf.com to discover more about the book and find advice on remote-first conferences.

Ultimately, what we want to achieve, whether it be through informal chats at the coffee machine, communities of practice, lunchtime talks, or internal conferences, is to help build and develop networks for informal knowledge sharing that can help support potential future collaborations. If, for example, there is a need to suddenly work with a different team, there is at least some level of trust already established between individuals within the organization.

Below is a table that breaks down multiple types of mechanisms for networking and knowledge sharing at different levels in the organization.

Type	Knowledge sharing type (targeted or diffuse)	Networking opportunity (yes or no)	Community (individuals, team, group, org wide)
Communities of practice	Diffuse	Yes	Group
Internal tech events	Diffuse	Yes	Org wide
Lunchtime talks	Diffuse	No	Group
Coffee breaks	—	Yes	Individuals
Enabling teams	Targeted	No	Team

Example

Throughout 2020–2021, numerous businesses and conference organizers had to adapt how they delivered their conferences from huge, physical, in-person events to remotely run online events.

A great example of this was the Engine Room conference put on by the *Financial Times*. Their goal was to primarily build connections and create space for conversation. It included education and some idea-sparking, but they really put a great deal of focus on sharing a space with the wider community at *Financial Times*. Feedback from their attendees was extremely positive.

Sarah Wells, then Technical Director for Operations and Reliability at the *Financial Times*, summarized some of their key learnings:[7]

- Use familiar tools: don't add unnecessary cognitive load.
- Keep it shorter and sharper: it's harder to hold people's attention remotely.
- Create space for hanging out: people don't get much chance to interact beyond their team when working remotely.
- Always strive for inclusivity.

Now Your Turn

Do you currently run any of the types of network-building events mentioned in this section? Did you used to have the water cooler and coffee machine chats, lunchtime talks, communities of practice, or internal conferences, but in the remote world, they have just stopped? Why not consider organizing a small event online where a few teams can talk about their work and discuss challenges with other members of the organization?

It doesn't need to be a large investment of time and effort. Start with a small group of people, perhaps a couple of teams or departments, while you evaluate how the format works. Then ask yourself these questions: Are there any obstacles, political or technical, that might get in the way of you doing this more broadly? What can you do to mitigate those issues to ensure everyone is able to take away valuable knowledge sharing and trust building?

Aim to keep the content as simple and easy as possible while you de-risk the delivery mechanism. After you have delivered a few sessions, begin to expand to a wider audience.

CHAPTER 3

Setting Team Boundaries

Inter-team trust and behavior dynamics change depending on the size of the group. It's important to avoid an "us and them" situation, so pay attention to the trust dynamics within and across teams and larger groups. This chapter provides some techniques for maintaining high trust within teams and groups in a remote-first world based on group size.

Group Trust Boundaries

When considering boundaries of teams and other groups within the organization, it is important to consider "group trust levels"—the amount of trust that can exist within groupings of a certain size. This is no different (but possibly harder) when it comes to remote-first teams, due to the lack of face-to-face contact. With high trust, groups can make decisions quickly and improve flow. However, there are well-recognized limits to trust that seem to relate to basic human evolutionary limits (like brain size).

The British anthropologist Robin Dunbar has done significant research on the size of social networks: the number of people with whom a person can have meaningful relationships. He found that an individual's social network size is typically in the order of one hundred to two hundred individuals. This research was undertaken on different groups of humans across many different countries and contexts, and there are similar-sized groupings in historical records too. For example, the typical size of a village in England in the Domesday Book census of 1086 (nearly one thousand years ago) was 150 people.

Robin Dunbar has also done research into online social networks, and what's really interesting is the same kind of trust boundaries—the same kind of social groupings—are present. A typical person maintains no more than about 150 meaningful relationships on social media (such as Facebook or Twitter). So even if you have five thousand Facebook friends, you actually tend to interact with only about 150. These trust boundaries, and how you can organize teams within them, are represented in the image below.

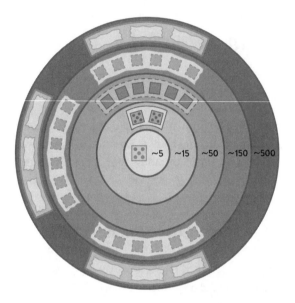

Figure 3.1: Scaling Teams Using Dunbar's Number

Source: Matthew Skelton and Manuel Pais, *Team Topologies: Organizing Business and Technology Teams for Fast Flow* (Portland, OR: IT Revolution, 2019).

READ MORE

Read more about Dunbar's number and trust boundaries in *Team Topologies* on pages 32–35.

But do these trust boundaries apply in a work context? Early in 2020, some new research by Emily Webber and Robin Dunbar found that these same trust boundaries are present inside organizations in the context of communities of practice (CoP), suggesting that other groups in a work context may also be affected. Specifically, CoP groups exhibited a similar "fractal" structure to that seen in other social contexts.

The research "suggests that professional work-oriented organizations may be subject to the same kinds of constraint imposed on human social organization by the social brain,"[1] meaning that the sizes of CoPs tended to group around the "Dunbar" trust boundaries of 5, 15, 50, 150, 500 people, etc., and—by extension—the social dynamics of different-sized CoPs will also be different.

The manufacturing company W. L. Gore has over ten thousand employees. For many years, W. L. Gore has operated a policy of limiting the size of each factory or office to 150 people in order to maintain high trust within that location, choosing to build an additional 150-person factory if they need to increase capacity. This was the company policy even before Robin Dunbar published his research on social group sizes, and it continues to help W. L.Gore be one of the most innovative manufacturers in the world.

Example: Military Groupings

There have been distinct group sizes in the military for hundreds and even thousands of years. Ben Ford, a former Royal Marines Commando (part of the elite UK military forces) and now a software consultant, describes "social inflection points," or group sizes, used in the military to enhance trust and operational effectiveness.[2] Ford maps the group sizes in the Royal Marines to anthropological equivalents, as shown in the table below:

People	Military name	Anthropological equivalent
8	Section	Hunting party
30–50	Troop	Tribe
100–150	Company	Village

The Section is the basic unit in the Royal Marines: eight people form a "single cohesive unit." The Troop is a collection of three Sections plus supporting units totalling around thirty to fifty people. This is the way Sections are coordinated to achieve larger objectives. A Company is a grouping of around three Troops with some supporting units and capabilities. At a larger scale, a Commando Unit is a grouping of three Company groups.

What's important is the fractal nature of these groupings: the patterns are self-similar at different scales. At each level, trust is maximized and there is no "us and them" within a grouping.

These kinds of trust boundaries have been effectively established by trial and error by the military over many, many hundreds of years in order to maximize trust and operational effectiveness. It's clear that these groupings map closely to the groupings that Robin Dunbar has found within social networks and have important implications for how we think about groupings of people inside organizations.

Now Your Turn

As we've seen in this section, for organizations to be highly effective, they need to look at trust boundaries when growing, when aligning teams to work, and when considering spheres of influence. Groups within an organization that grow in size beyond one of these trust boundaries are likely to have difficulty maintaining cohesion and trust, leading to an "us and them" attitude and reduced effectiveness.

Trust Boundaries Exercise

Consider your current organization or another organization that you know well. Create a list or map of the different groups of people within the organization and the number of people in each group. Consider business units, divisions, departments, value streams, teams, and so on. How many people are inside each grouping?

Now use the Dunbar trust boundary numbers or "social inflection points" (e.g, 5, 15, 50, 150, 500, 1,500, 5,000, etc.). Which groupings within the organization are far from the Dunbar trust boundaries? For example, a department with 300 people would be very far from the two nearest Dunbar boundaries of 150 and 500.

Next, ask what the culture is like inside groupings with "non-Dunbar" numbers of people. What are the trust dynamics? Which groupings could be split at Dunbar boundaries to help increase trust within the groupings?

Use the below template to help assess the size of groups in an organization in relation to Dunbar number trust boundaries. Groups that are slightly smaller than the trust boundary are likely to have good trust in relation to the number of people; groups that are somewhat larger than the trust boundary are likely to have problems with low trust in relation to the number of people. These groups are candidates for splitting into smaller groups.

Group name	Group size (people)	Closest trust boundary (15/50/500)	Likely trust problems? (Y/N)

Online Space Setup

Applying the ideas of group trust boundaries to physical space is fairly straightforward: when a room, floor, building, or location reaches and exceeds a certain trust boundary size, expect trust dynamics to change. Expect "us and them" mentalities to emerge. However, we also need to apply these same principles to online spaces, especially chat tools and online documentation tools like wikis.

Too often, an online communication tool resembles something like a giant, open-plan office with people shouting across the building and expecting people to hear all the details. Communication in online spaces must be designed and nurtured for best outcomes.

What does this mean in practice? Much like how W. L. Gore builds a new factory when the number of people reaches 150, consider managing online spaces in a similar way. When the size of an online space reaches a trust boundary (such as 50 or 150 people), instead of adding more people to the same online space, create a new space. Each online space grouping should have people with a shared focus on a related flow of change.

Exactly what the boundary for this grouping is may differ from organization to organization: sometimes a 150-person boundary might be a single channel or channel group, and sometimes the boundary might be an entire workspace. The key thing is to design the online space with trust boundaries in mind. It's important to note that each separate online space should also relate to a flow of change, not to different job "functions" within the organization.

Good candidates for separate online spaces would map to streams of change (or families of streams of change). Let's say an organization provides services for buying, selling, and leasing vehicles. The separate online spaces might map to private vehicle sales, commercial vehicle sales, and vehicle leasing, corresponding to the three separate business lines within the organization. Every team involved in the private vehicle sales business line would be in the same online space: engineering, IT, sales, marketing, HR, legal, etc. This helps to focus the organization on a fast flow of change rather than functional specialisms. (Note: It is not recommended to create separate online spaces for functional specialisms like HR, legal, marketing, IT, etc., because that approach works against a fast flow of change.)

In Figure 3.2, we can see how we might create and align online spaces with groupings of related teams. For example, it would likely make sense to have a dedicated online space for each group of teams working on the same business area or value stream. We might also want to have a dedicated online space for all the teams that are part of an internal platform group, for example.

In this example, the separate online spaces help to remind people of the different boundaries within the architecture and therefore the boundaries within teams. We can still have shared channels between different online spaces to help create slightly porous boundaries between these spaces. Some examples include Slack Connect's shared channels and Slack's Enterprise Grid product, which allows for multiple workspaces to exist under one overarching oganizational container. This means explicit cross-space communication can still take place for sporadic needs across boundaries.

The inherent trust inside different organizations may be very different due to culture and practices, so one organization may find that online spaces of 500 people work well, but another organization may find more benefit in restricting each online space to only 150 people (See Figure 3.3). In short, optimize for trust within online spaces. Do not be tempted to optimize for manageability, ease of billing, or ease of observation across multiple groups, as this can impede flow.

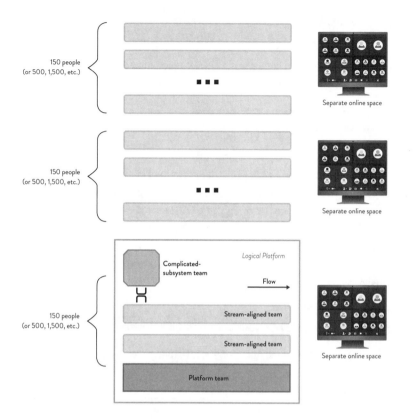

Figure 3.2: Separate Online Spaces Aligned to Groupings of Teams and Trust Boundaries

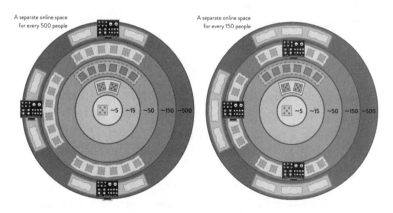

Figure 3.3: Online Spaces of Different Sizes According to the
Organization's Culture and Practices

READ MORE

Read more about setting up team-first physical and online/virtual spaces in *Team Topologies,* pages 50–55.

Example: Auto Trader

Auto Trader is the UK's largest digital automotive marketplace. Starting life as a local classified magazine in 1977, it has grown and evolved alongside its customers. In 2013, it successfully completed the transition from a print title to a fully digital marketplace. Prior to the COVID-19 pandemic, Auto Trader had invested time and money in a first-class physical workplace in Manchester, UK. Interestingly, while many organizations consider having a single collaboration tool as an imperative, Auto Trader uses both Slack and Microsoft Teams simultaneously to complement each tool's strengths.

READ MORE

This is detailed in the Auto Trader case study in *Team Topologies* on pages 53–55.

As may be expected from an organization that considered its team working practices carefully, Auto Trader has focused on optimizing tools and working practices to get the most out of remote and hybrid working. Andy Humphrey, Head of Customer Operations at Auto Trader UK, explains:

> We've worked hard to adapt the way we use communication tools for times when remote working is mandatory and where hybrid working both in and out of the office has become the norm.
>
> This is a challenge not just for a team's or individual's productivity, but to ensure our well-being is supported and we can continue to build the relationship and connections that are so important to our organizational culture.
>
> We now heavily use Microsoft Teams for video calls, and it has developed into our main company live video broadcast tool to support the Auto Trader community—with every employee invited. For exam-

ple, we had a bi-weekly update from the CEO and our leadership team in the midst of the pandemic, plus weekly talks where people presented different areas of work/interest. Microsoft Teams was also used for:

- The de facto replacement for team meetings such as stand-ups, retrospectives, kick-offs, etc.
- Department or tribe gatherings and events.
- Recruitment processes, including conducting interviews online where lockdown restricted face-to-face meetings or geography makes in-person meetings difficult.
- Customer meetings such as video calls and live broadcasts to build relationships and help training and communication.

Slack was heavily used within the technology department before the pandemic, but now its reach is wider across the organization and product areas. Slack is used in a number of different ways at Auto Trader, including:

- Interest based networks: We have a lot of communities of interest where people can join together in their workplace based on shared passions, characteristics, or life experiences, e.g., #sustainability-network; #womens-network; #social-mobility. These working groups are open to all but tend to have at least two leaders and often executive sponsors.
- Social/well-being: We have regular online reading groups, film clubs, Friday quizzes, pictures of pets, coffee chat areas, and even a personal trainer running regular online exercise classes. Again, these are open to all.
- Business focus networks: We have Slack channels for project areas and business-focused areas—like different teams sitting to-gether to focus on a customer group, such as leasing, new cars, etc.
- Team networks: Regular conversation—from updates on work, getting help with problems, organizing lunch rotas, just saying "hi" and "bye," etc.—with your team is really important, especially for teams who are now working apart.
- Dynamic groups: Channels spin up for an incident (war room) or other temporary need, where previously we might have grabbed a few people and gone into a meeting room.

Often the needs of these Slack groups means that we need to branch off to other tools and formats for meetings, events, and working groups. But Slack is the place you look for updates and go to show your interest, contribute, and find out what's going on.

The numbers involved in these chat groups can vary wildly from over five hundred in some channels where everyone wants an update to fewer than ten for smaller teams or niche interests![3]

The considered approach to online spaces continued at Auto Trader during the following year. In August 2021, Karl Stoney, principal engineer at Auto Trader, tweeted about some updates to their Slack integration that enabled the dynamic creation of Slack groups based upon a service metadata file that is stored in each product repository. It also maintains an Active Directory group, which is useful for assigning permissions, single sign-on (SSO), etc.[4]

Prior to implementing this, each of these things represented a separate task to be undertaken for each of over 450 services, which, in an organization that often has new starters, caused significant toil. This is a great example of how automation can eliminate some of the more repetitive and mundane daily tasks, introduce consistency, and substantially improve productivity.

READ MORE

Read more about practices at Auto Trader in *Team Topologies*, pages 97–99.

Now Your Turn: *Online Space Assessment*

Consider your current organization or another organization that you know well. Identify the different tools used for online spaces within the organization. These are typically chat tools (such as Slack, Microsoft Teams, Twist, IRC, Yammer, Skype, etc.) but could be other immersive tools too.

For each separate instance of one of these tools (where an "instance" means different administrators or different permission sets), list the total number of members. Then, for each channel in that space, list the number of members of each channel or chat within that space. For each instance, and for each channel within that instance, determine whether the number of channel members is close to a trust boundary or whether the size falls between two trust boundaries.

Groups that are slightly smaller than a trust boundary are likely to have good trust in relation to the number of people; groups that are somewhat larger than a trust boundary are likely to have problems with low trust in relation to the number of people. These groups are candidates for splitting into smaller groups. Consider even splitting some of the online space instances into multiple smaller spaces to help maintain higher trust within the space.

Here are some templates to help you assess your online spaces.

SEPARATE ONLINE SPACE (INSTANCES)				
Online space name	Online space URL	Tool providing the service	Number of members	Likely trust problems? (Y/N)

CHANNELS WITHIN AN ONLINE SPACE				
Channel name	Members (# of people)	Closest trust boundary (15, 50, 150, etc.)	Number of members	Likely trust problems? (Y/N)

RESOURCE

You can download this template at GitHub.com/TeamTopologies/Online-Space-Assessment.

Team-Focused Conventions for Chat Tools

There are many different chat tools available for remote-first working, and most organizations are using a chat tool (or several) these days. However, simply providing all staff access to a chat tool is only the first step in making remote-first working a success.

Too many organizations allow a kind of free rein within the chat tool, with little or no consistency about channel names, display names, the meanings of emoji, or even etiquette. This can rapidly lead to the chat tool becoming both essential to watch (in case you miss a vital message) and incredibly confusing and difficult to use.

For effective remote work, some chat tool conventions are needed. The virtual space inside the chat tool needs to be predictable and discoverable. Arbitrary channel names like *#homepage_discussion*, *#increase-conversions*, and *#ninjas* make it difficult to know where to go to discuss a topic. If this is combined with multiple private channels, finding the right people to speak to is a game of cat and mouse.

Instead, define a set of conventions that improve predictability and discoverability. For example, include the team name and type of team in the channel name for the team's main outward-facing chat channel.

- **#streamteam-green**: the public channel for the stream-aligned team "Green"
- **#streamteam-blue**: the public channel for the stream-aligned team "Blue"
- **#platformteam-data**: the public channel for the platform team "Data"
- **#platformteam-infra**: the public channel for the platform team "Infra"
- **#enablingteam-k8s**: the public channel for the enabling team "k8s"

The three team interaction modes from *Team Topologies* can help to further increase the clarity of purpose for teams working together.

- **Collaboration**: two teams working together for a defined discovery period to achieve a specific goal)
- **X-as-a-Service**: one team provides something as a service, another team consumes)

- **Facilitating**: one team helps another to detect capability gaps or increase skills and awareness)

> The Introduction and Chapter 4 of this workbook have more details on the three team interaction modes.

Furthermore, it can be hugely helpful to have channel names that make it clear where to get support or help for common or shared infrastructure or tools:

- **#support-environments**: the support channel for environments
- **#support-logging**: the support channel for logging

This makes it easy for people to "self-serve" and discover the best place to ask a question or ask for help. Once the channel is found, to facilitate X-as-a-Service interaction, consider adding bookmarks to the channel header that provide instructions on how to consume the services offered by the team. Most chat tools also provide a simple way to standardize the structure of requests coming into the team. For example, teams can use Slack Workflow builder templates.

Similarly, set some conventions around the display name that shows in the chat for each person. A display name of "Jim" or "sara_b" provides much less context than something like "Jim Ngo (Infra Platform Team)" or "Sara Brown (Green Stream Team)." With the more descriptive display names, we have immediate context for who a person is and how they are related to us in the organization.

Example

For example, a stream-aligned team might be interacting with two other teams: a test automation enabling team (using facilitating interaction) and a face recognition complicated-subsystem team (using collaboration interaction). In this case, there would be two temporary chat tool channels that are named to clarify these interactions:

- **#testautomation-facilitating-green**: for communication between the test automation enabling team and the green stream-aligned team in the context of the facilitating interaction taking place

- **#facerecognition-collaboration-green**: for communication between the face recognition complicated-subsystem team and the green stream-aligned team in the context of the collaboration interaction taking place

The channel names make it easy to discover where to hold discussions between the teams involved. The discussions in these channels relate only to the interaction between the teams involved, so the chat is focused and not "polluted" with other unrelated discussions.

Now Your Turn

Look at the channel names in the chat tool within your current organization and choose ten to twenty channel names as examples. How well do the channel names convey the purpose of the channel? What combination of information (such as team name, team type, and interaction mode) in the channel name would help to clarify the purpose of the channel? What channel names would make it easy to discover where interactions between two teams are taking place?

> **RESOURCE**
>
> Use the Online Space Assessment template shown in the previous section or download at GitHub.com/TeamTopologies/Online-Space-Assessment.

CHAPTER 4

Purposeful Interactions

"**M**ore collaboration" is often suggested as a solution to ineffective organizations; but, in reality, collaboration needs to be carefully curated to avoid unintended effects and cognitive overload. This chapter explains some techniques to use to help make team interactions more purposeful (whether remote or in person), including detecting ineffective team interactions.

Team Interaction Modes:
A Review

As we discuss in *Team Topologies*, it is a common myth that we just need to communicate and collaborate more—just tell everybody everything! Unfortunately, it is not quite that simple.

Research by Harvard Business School published in 2018 found that in a knowledge work context, where there is discovery and innovation taking place, organizations that had everyone talking to everyone else all the time actually performed worse than in situations where teams or groups of people communicated and collaborated on a more occasional basis.[1] This supports the idea that we actually need to create more purposeful interactions between teams.

In a remote work context, we tend to see the opposite: intentional communications between teams can drastically diminish in favor of a "broadcasting" approach to information sharing.

Regardless of whether we're over or under communicating, we can enable effective teams by being more purposeful about the type of communication and the type of interactions that we have with other groups in the organization, and, therefore, we can achieve better outcomes. The key is to have well-defined interactions between each of the teams whether they are colocated or remote.

In *Team Topologies*, we define three core team interaction modes:

Collaboration: two teams working together for a specific period of time in order to achieve a well-defined outcome.

X-as-a-Service: one team providing and one team consuming something.

Facilitating: one team helping another team to improve or discover something.

Collaboration between two teams over a short period of time can yield effective results. However, if that collaboration continues over a longer period of time, it is probably less effective. Collaboration between two teams with different skills over a long period can be quite intense and can suggest that there is potentially a missing capability or functionality within one of the teams. In this situation, we should look for ways to reduce the dependency between those teams that causes a recurring need for collaboration.

X-as-a-Service is a more long-lived interaction mode, provided that the service being supplied is (or continues to be) easily consumed by the receiving team. It is the consumption of the service by the receiving team that will determine whether the service can be considered a good fit for X-as-a-Service. However, it is important for the providing team to continually listen to feedback from the receiving teams and ensure that what worked before is still working now. They should be testing whether the service boundary is in the right place.

To determine this, both teams should try answering the following questions: If the business context has changed, do we need to shift where the boundary of responsibility lies for that thing that is being consumed? Should we be doing more as a team or should the service provider be doing more work? Both the providing team and consuming teams should always be thinking about whether the current service being provided is still the right thing. Is this interaction still the right kind of interaction? It was six months ago, but is it still?

The use of the facilitating interaction mode, where one team helps another team, is similar to that of collaboration. Short effective periods, maybe two to three weeks, of facilitation between the two teams is probably a good thing. But if that facilitating interaction is still going on after six months, it suggests something isn't quite right.

In Figure 4.1, you can see that we have captured a snapshot in time of the current interaction modes between a set of fictitious teams.

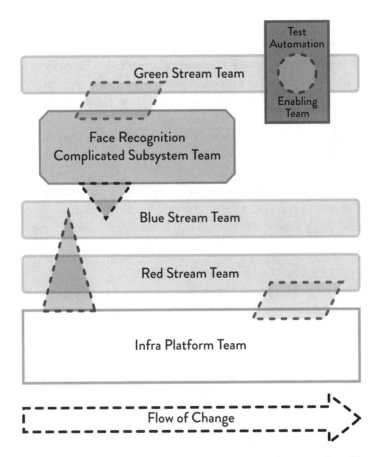

Figure 4.1: A Snapshot in Time of the Interactions Happening between a Set of Teams

It is clear that Green Stream Team is currently collaborating with the complicated subsystem team. We should expect this to be a short-term collaboration in order to define and develop a future X-as-a-Service interaction allowing the Green Stream Team to deliver value faster in the future.

We can also see that both the Blue Stream Team and the Red Stream Team consume services from the Infra Platform Team, but the Red Stream Team is also collaborating with the Infra Platform Team. Again, this may be to develop another service that the Red Stream Team could consume in the future.

In this case, the Green Stream Team is also receiving some facilitation from the Test Automation Enabling Team, which may be to help with the integrating tests in a CI/CD pipeline or kickstarting an automation test suite, for example.

The important thing to remember at this stage is that this figure is just a snapshot. This is not a static model for the organization to follow mindlessly from now and into the future. It may represent what is happening today or perhaps what is expected to happen in two months from now, but it is essential to recognize that it represents a moment in time rather than a fixed team design.

Diagrams like the one in Figure 4.1 are useful as visual prompts to help promote robust discussions around how teams are currently interacting or how the team interaction modes could or should change after a period of time. However, it is important for each team to recognize and record their current interactions as well as their expected future interactions, and then to make these easily available for others within the organization to see via their team API.

> Please see Chapter 2 of this workbook for more details and examples of the Team API.

Example

There are two sections of the team API that are useful in helping to determine the necessary team interaction modes between teams: "teams we currently interact with" and "teams we expect to interact with soon." Both are in the tables on the following page.

We can see in the examples provided on the next page that the team API has been completed by this team at a specific moment in time. They have captured that they are currently interacting with the Test Automation Enabling Team and that they are currently using the facilitating interaction mode. Their stated purpose or goal is to gain a better understanding of test automation for iOS.

This interaction occurs one day per week and is planned to last approximately two months. During this period, the team is also going to be collaborating with the Video Calls Stream Team. The purpose of their interaction is to determine how to handle authentication workflow errors in the Video Calls service. There is an expectation that this will require interactions of up to two hours per day over a three-week period.

Being clear about the purpose and interaction type enables us to ask questions like: Is the interaction truly one of collaboration? Does it feel right? Is the projected duration correct? Does it look like we are going to need much more time? If it is looking that way, what is that telling us?

Teams we currently interact with:

Team name	Interaction mode	Purpose	Duration	Interaction location
Test Automation Enabling Team	Facilitating	Understand test automation and data mgmt examples for iOS	2 months (from Mar 30 to May 29, 1 day per week)	Miro
Video Calls Stream Team	Collaboration	Define workflow for authentication errors in Video Calls service	3 weeks (from Apr 13 to Apr 30, 2h per day)	Zoom

Teams we expect to interact with soon:

Team name	Interaction mode	Purpose	Duration	Interactin location
Call Admin Stream Team	Collaboration	Clarify and test authentication permissions for new Call Admin stand-alone app	2 weeks (from May 1 to May 14, 2h per day)	Microsoft Teams

Just because it is taking longer than expected doesn't mean that an interaction is necessarily good or bad, but it is a signal that we should listen for and pay attention to. Perhaps the original problem was misunderstood. Or maybe one of the teams has a gap in skills or capabilities that prevents collaboration from being effective. The key is that we are defining and observing the interactions, making it much easier to have sensible conversations about the results of the interaction.

Now Your Turn

If you haven't already created a team API, as defined in Chapter 2 of this workbook, now might be a good time to create one.

Starting with one of your teams, think about which other teams they are currently interacting with and ask yourself the following questions:

- What is the type of the interaction: collaboration, facilitating, or X-as-a-Service?
- What is the purpose of the interaction?
- How many hours or days per week should the teams be interacting?
- What should be the duration of the interaction?

Make sure you capture the answers to these questions in the team API artifact and set a reminder to revisit each interaction some time in the near future, maybe in a month or two, to check that the captured interactions are still relevant. Repeat this with each of your teams.

Listening to Team Interactions

Difficulties or awkwardness in team interactions can be used as a kind of sensing mechanism to help evolve the organization in the right way. For example, a platform team has produced a new service to help stream-aligned teams. If those stream-aligned teams struggle to understand the service or require a lot of help to use that service, then perhaps the service is a bit too complicated. Maybe the developer experience isn't good enough or the abstraction point is not quite right. In this case, we may require the help of an enabling team to work out where to put the abstraction by moving the API responsibility.

In the previous section, we defined and captured how these interactions should happen, which allows us to listen for when they go wrong. This can be a leading indicator for potential architectural and software delivery problems that we can spot, enabling us to identify and address them as early as possible.

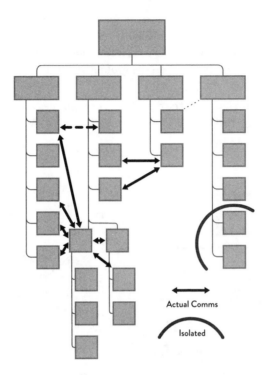

Figure 4.2: Org Chart with Lines of Actual Communication

The blocks connected by thin lines in Figure 4.2 show a typical organizational chart with a very hierarchical view that does not truly represent the communication that occurs within the organization. The actual communication lines that happen within an organization are shown in thick lines with arrows. People from different departments communicate with each other. At the same time, some parts of the organization might be isolated (shown with the curved line on the right-hand side).

Organizational charts like these are not fundamentally problematic as they can be very useful for certain situations, such as regulatory reporting. However, the problem with the organizational chart is that for a lot of knowledge work and discovery activities, we cannot have communication only happening up and down the different branches.

This problem is explained very well in the book *Team of Teams* by former US Army General Stanley McChrystal. The book centers around a time when the US Army was in Iraq fighting Al Qaeda. It describes how the Army was organized very hierarchically (like the org chart in Figure 4.2). However, they were facing a threat that had a very different decision-making and execution structure, which meant they had to radically change their organization to be able to respond to the situation on the ground at a much faster pace than the hierarchy could ever achieve.

You can see in Figure 4.3 the difference between the communication structure that the Army had been designed for versus the reality of what they were facing.

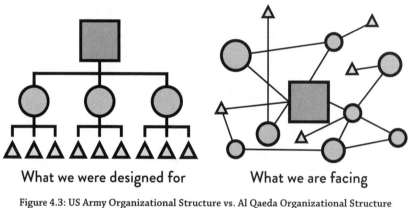

Figure 4.3: US Army Organizational Structure vs. Al Qaeda Organizational Structure

McChrystal et al., *Team of Teams: New Rules of Engagement for a Complex World* (NY: Penguin, 2015).

The key thing is that we need to let real needs drive the interactions between teams, not formal processes or organizational chart decisions. By "real needs," we mean meeting the needs of customers and people who are actually using the software systems. A focus on flow will help meet those needs as effectively and quickly as possible.

This focus on flow—guided by Team Topologies principles like decoupling, domain-centric boundaries, limiting cognitive load, and so forth—helps to make asynchronous, remote work happen more effectively precisely because people in separate locations have the context, trust, and focus to be able to work effectively: partly independently and partly synchronizing on key decisions and explorations.

We want to avoid situations where the organizational chart restricts communication between teams. Instead, use the well-defined interactions and team APIs to make clear why there is a need to communicate with other teams in order to build different parts of the system.

In the context of remote work, it is too easy to accidentally fall into a swamp of direct private messages and people contacting specific individuals because chat tools make this possible. If the work were office-based, people would have to leave their desk and walk to the person. This higher bar often helps people pause and consider their communication first. To avoid the tempting swamp of direct messages in the context of remote work, we need clearly defined interaction models.

Example

Let's look at an example. Imagine a situation where a stream-aligned team in an organization is interacting with a platform team that provides cloud infrastructure as a service, as in the team API below.

Team name	Interaction mode	Purpose	Duration	Notes
Infra Platform Team	X-as-a-Service	Cloud infrastructure on-demand services	Ongoing	We seem to be spending a lot of time reinventing the wheel and researching how to do things, the developer experience and documentation could be improved

However, when the stream-aligned team assesses whether the service provided by the platform team is easy to use and consume, they note that the current service seems to require that the stream-aligned team spend a lot of time researching how to get things done, and the documentation is not easily discoverable and consumable.

This suggests that the platform team might not really be listening to the needs of its users. Time should be spent improving that part of the service to reduce the cognitive load required from the stream-aligned team today.

While there could be a number of reasons to explain this situation (which will require further investigation), it is important to note that this type of awkward interaction could signify that the platform team may require the help of an enabling team to better understand the platform users (the stream-aligned teams).

Now Your Turn

Take a look at some of the team interactions that are happening within your organization. Make a record of what the expected interactions should be using in the team API (see Chapter 2 of this workbook) and question whether these expectations are being met: Are teams spending a long time trying to use a given service or component? Is there a lack of interaction between teams that should be collaborating to reduce their dependencies? Does work spend a lot of time waiting in queues? Is the team throughput slowing down?

> ### RESOURCE
>
> Download the team API template: GitHub.com/TeamTopologies/Team-API-Template.

Once you have identified potential awkward interactions, think about what might be causing them. This could include things like the service or component not being well specified or too difficult to use. Or maybe the team is missing a capability, doesn't understand the value of the collaboration, or the boundary that the teams are trying to bridge is too large.

> ### READ MORE
>
> Read more about awkward team interactions in *Team Topologies* on pages 150–151.

Clarify Communication Purpose and Channels

In order for an organization to be effective, especially in a remote context, it is essential for the purpose and channel of any communication to be clear and obvious.

In Chapter 2 of this workbook, we discussed how we can use consistent naming conventions in tools such as Slack or Mircosoft Teams to help channels become more discoverable. But it is equally important to ensure consistency of purpose for those channels. Should a channel be public or private? Should it support a community or team, or focus on a specific topic?

Public channels should be created to enable people outside of a team to ask questions to the team rather than to individuals within the team. Doing this helps reinforce the concept of team-based ownership and reduce occurrences of people reaching out to individuals, which can be disruptive for both those individuals as well as the team. (Of course, each team will need their own private channel for internal discussions.)

Other than team-specific channels, another type you may want to consider is the community channel. These channels allow people in the communities within your organization to talk to each other, as well as for external people to ask questions to the community. Communities tend to form around areas of practice, such as UX, testing, architecture, or specific technologies and tools.

Another type of channel is a topic channel. This type of channel could be short or long lived and should be focused around trying to solve a specific issue or an immediate problem/incident that is being investigated. After the problem has been solved, a topic channel will typically be archived so that it no longer clutters the channel list but is still accessible if needed at a later date.

It is important to define usage guidelines for tools such as Slack and Microsoft Teams so everyone in the organization has a reference for recommended good practices when using them. Consider having a "public by default" policy to help provide the best opportunity to learn from any discussions but curate the experience to ensure that, where appropriate, people's focus is narrowed to the relevant information that is useful to them.

Example

A company in the telecommunications sector has over 120 teams across three countries. The company uses Slack for internal communication and aims to make it easy and straightforward to "discover the best place to communicate" through channel naming conventions. Some conventions that seem to work include grouping by Tribe (a collection of teams), grouping by community of practice, grouping by incident, and grouping by management initiative. This results in channels named like this:

Channel name	Interpretation	Notes
#tribe-payments-card-management	The Card Management team within the Payments tribe	Search for #tribe- finds all Tribe-related channels
#tribe-payments-cde	The CDE (card data environment) team within the Payments tribe	Search for #tribe-payments finds all channels relating to the Payments Tribe
#tribe-myprofile-orderhistory	The Order History team within the My Profile tribe	Search for #myprofile finds all channels relating to the My Profile, including all the Tribe Channels
#cop-ux	The UX Community of Practice	Search for #cop finds all channels relating to communities of practice
#cop-testability	The Testability Community of Practice	Search for #test finds all channels relating to testing, testability, etc. and so discovers this CoP
#in-67351-2021-09-15	Incident channel for incident number 67351 that started on 15 September 2021	Search for #in- finds all channels relating to incidents
#mgt-learning-vle	Discussion around VLE (virtual learning environment) as part of the learning initiatives	Search for #mgt finds all channels relating to management initiatives

For discoverability to work well, channels typically need to be public (or searchable organization-wide, rather than open to the outside world). Keeping channels discoverable requires some effort in design and curation of the chat workspace.

Now Your Turn

Take a random sample of twenty to thirty channel names in the chat communication tool used within your organization. Can you decipher the purpose of each channel? Could a new member of staff decipher the purpose of the channels? What kind of naming schemes appear to be in use? Do different parts of the organization use different naming conventions? How "discoverable" are the right places to have conversations?

Ensuring Clarity of Purpose of Platforms and Services

The team API is useful for surfacing information about a team's purpose and how that team interacts with other teams, but it is equally important for platforms and services within the organization to have a clearly defined interface that speaks to people and allows them to understand how they can interact with them.

In *Team Topologies*, we discuss the introduction of a *thinnest viable platform* (TVP), which can be as simple as a wiki page that captures key information about how to consume external services.

READ MORE

Read more about thinnest viable platforms in *Team Topologies* on pages 101, 184, and 188.

Once there is a need for a dedicated platform team responsible for the TVP, we need to expose the "interfaces" to that team. You can start by detailing your thinnest viable platform, including information such as:

- hours of operation
- brief description of the service(s) provided
- documentation for onboarding
- examples of typical response times
- road map of features being developed
- preferred ways to contact the support team
- details about communication channels, e.g., chat tools, email, phone

The thinnest viable platform is effectively a socio-technical API around a given service. It is not just the code-level API; it is the connection that speaks to human beings, allowing them to understand how they can interact with the platform.

Example: Equal Experts & ITV

Equal Experts has a great example of a Slack usage guide that you can use as a basis for defining your own (see the resources below). In their guide, they outline principles and guidelines to help users get the most shared benefit out of the tool. But it is also evolving as the organization evolves (it is not static). They used the following principles when creating their usage guidelines:[2]

- Give everyone the bigger picture by making information and conversations public
  » Widen people's context
  » Make channels public by default, it provides the greatest opportunity for others to learn from any discussion and it documents tribal knowledge.
- Increase the signal to noise ratio of the information and conversations
  » Narrow people's focus
  » Ensure people are reading information that is relevant and useful to them
  » Efficiently use people's time
- Respect the amount of information anyone can tolerate reading
  » Do not overwhelm people with a high volume of messages that they are expected to read
  » Avoid communication burnout
- Optimize for the whole of the global organization rather than local optimizations for parts of the organization
  » Avoid creating a disjointed experience for people by focusing on overall simplicity rather than local simplicity

RESOURCE

You can see their full usage guide here: GitHub.com/EqualExperts/Slack-Guide.

They have also created an open-source tool called the Equal Experts Gardener Tool, which curates and maintains channels to ensure their users have a good communication experience. This tool is used to automatically archive inactive channels to help improve the visibility of conversations and makes it easier for new joiners to find channels that are relevant to them.

Another example comes from ITV. Tom Clark, their head of common platform at the time, talked frankly about some of the issues they encountered when trying to develop their internal platform that supported all of their product teams at the DevOps Enterprise Summit–London in 2019.[3] After realizing that version one of the common platform focused mainly on infrastructure hosting rather than helpful services for product development, they staged an intervention with the goal to "provide a brilliant hosting and development platform."[4] In order to achieve this, they reached out to their customers (the product teams) and asked the question, "What can we do better to support you?"

One of the key responses was to be more transparent and communicate what they were doing more clearly. So, as they embarked on version two of the platform development, they ensured that they set up a public road map and backlog, and they publicized its existence, allowing anyone to see progress. They created a specific Slack channel for the project, allowing other members of the team to join the conversation. They also set up a contributors group, allowing a mechanism for constant feedback from their customers.

All of this enabled the team to create a new, compelling platform version that resulted in Dave Smith, a principal developer at ITV, sending an email to his team encouraging them to use the new platform: "The performance is better, it's cheaper to run, the config is nicer, the deployment timers are delightful and the scaling is sublime."[5]

Obviously, there was more to the development of the platform than just the communication channels, but being transparent and engaging with customers of the platform in a focused and relevant way was a key contributor to its success.

Now Your Turn

Take a look at the channels in Slack or Microsoft Teams (or other chat tools) that you are currently using within your organization. Are they focused and relevant? Or are people bombarded with messages and notifications that they simply do not care about? Are people likely to unsubscribe from channels because they are too noisy?

Consider how you might create channels for teams that enable public communication with the whole team combined with private channels for the teams to engage in private conversations.

- Does it make sense to create channels around certain communities?
- Would the introduction of temporary, topic-specific channels help keep communication concise?
- If a new person is onboarded to your team, how easy would it be for them to learn which channels are relevant to the work they will be doing?
- Would the introduction of a Slack usage guide be beneficial within your organization to help keep remote communication consistent among all users?

Think about some of the platforms or services within your organization.

- How easy is it for people to discover what it is and how they should interact with it?
- How are you currently making that information consumable?
- Are there ways in which it could be improved?

You can use the thinnest viable platform template provided below as a basis to describe them.

Example Wiki Page: Thinnest Viable Platform Template

A simple but comprehensive wiki page provides a single point of entry for anyone wanting to know more about a service, report an issue, or find out the current status, road map, and so on. In this example for a thinnest viable platform, each team responsible for a platform service should answer the questions and fill in the details below. Repeat the Service Details section for each service that the team builds and runs.

(Thin) Platform Wiki

- Platform hours of operation: _____

Service details

- Short service description/purpose: _____

- Live status page: _____

Documentation

- Link to onboarding documentation: _____

- Link to service interface documentation: _____

- Here's a simple example of service usage: _____

Response times

- Responsible platform team name: _____

- Platform team response time for major incidents: _____

- Platform team response time for other incidents: _____

- Platform team response time for support: _____

- Platform team response time for feedback:_____

Road map

- Link to service road map: _____

Communication Channels

To report a possible incident contact exclusively via:

- Slack channel: _____

- Phone number: _____

To ask for support or provide feedback, contact via any of these:

- Slack Channel: _____

- Email: _____

- Phone: _____

- Office hours: (Day and time of the week) _____

RESOURCE

You can download this template at GitHub.com/TeamTopologies/Thin-Platform-Template.

CHAPTER 5

Next Steps

After exploring the patterns in this workbook, you may be looking for further techniques and approaches to try to help make a remote-first approach work well. This chapter gives some suggestions for further activities and patterns to adopt within your organization to make remote-first, team-centric work as effective as possible.

Design and Conduct a Developer Experience Platform Survey

One of the most important aspects of developing and running an internal platform of any kind is the continual "steering" of the platform features and usability by feedback from internal customers (engineering teams that use the platform). Two techniques that work well to shape the feedback from developers and other engineers are a platform survey and user personas for internal customers.

Internal Platform Survey

To begin with, ask a few simple questions about the usability and experience of using the internal platform. Send the form to various internal customers (developers and other engineers).

Below is a starter survey template for the developer experience. (This is the same form you can use to assess team cognitive load, as dicussed in Chapter 1, but now used in a different context. Given that one of the main purposes of a platform—in a Team Topologies sense—is to reduce cognitive load on teams using the platform, this should not be a surprise!)

Engineering Experience Feedback

With this survey, we want to assess how easy/hard you find it to build, test, run, and support the services your team is responsible for.

Note: answers will not be used in any kind of evaluation/review/appraisal context. Results will be aggregated at the team level.

Answer each question on a scale of 1 (very poor) to 5 (very good).

1. How is the experience of building your services? Things to consider: Is building a clear and repeatable task? Is it fast "enough"? What happens when builds fail? Are failures easy to diagnose?
2. How is the experience of testing your services? Things to consider: Is testing a clear and repeatable task? Is it fast "enough"? What happens when tests fail? Are failures easy to diagnose? Are test environments adequate? Are test environments easy to access/ spin up/clean up/inject test data?
3. How is the experience of deploying your services? Things to consider: Are deployments a clear and repeatable task? Do you know what the deployment strategy is? What happens when deployments fail? Is it possible and straightforward to rollback a failed deployment? Do you have access to the necessary logs to understand why a deployment failed and/or its current status?
4. How is the experience of operating your services? Things to consider: Do you know how each service is being monitored and have access to the data? Are adequate alerts (few false positives) being sent? Are logs and information accessible and easy to find? Are data flows across services relatively easy to follow?
5. How is the experience of being on call for your services? Things to consider: Do you know what the incident response procedure is? Do you feel you have enough experience (either real or simulated) to deal with incidents without high levels of stress? Do you know who to reach out to for help during an incident when you're on call? Would you be anxious about a 3 a.m. outage? What about an incident in a service that hasn't been modified for months or years?
6. Would you like to comment on your overall engineering experience?

For an example of a more advanced approach to platform surveys, see the excellent 2018 QCon presentation by Justin Kitagawa,[1] Senior Director of Engineering at Twilio, where he explains the approach they use to assess and improve the effectiveness of their internal platform. Twilio uses net promoter scores (NPS)—a technique common in consumer sales and marketing—to gauge how well the platform is perceived by internal customers.

Internal User Personas

Work with the user experience (UX) specialists in your organization to define and, most importantly, validate a set of user personas for internal customers (developers and other engineers). As with any user personas, it is vitally important to validate your assumptions with real users. Use this checking process to adjust your expectations about what needs to be built or provided to customers.

The simplest version of user personas is to characterize the goals and frustrations of each type of developer or engineer working with the platform: What do they want to achieve? And what do they find difficult?

Define Naming and Usage Conventions for Chat Tools

In a remote-first world, the chat tool becomes the online space in which work becomes coordinated. An online space that is clear to navigate and safe to use leads to better outcomes for teams.

Work through the suggestions in Chapter 3 of this workbook around naming conventions and usage of your chat tool. The aim is to create the conditions so a healthy dialogue can emerge to curate or nurture a good approach to the use of the online space around the chat tool. Do not be tempted to "design" everything up front: allow some patterns to emerge.

You may need to rework some of the channels or conventions after you introduce concepts like the team API, but that's fine. The organization needs to become adept at modifying the conventions of the online space as the organization grows (or shrinks) and meets new challenges.

Focus on discoverability or predictability: How easy is it for a new person to discover or predict the channels that they should join? Can you use some "bots" to help with onboarding and suggestions? Chat tool ecosystems typically have several options for automated onboarding help using bots.

Use the Team API with Multiple Teams to Define and Clarify Team Boundaries

In the remote-first world, teams benefit even more from defining the boundaries of their work since there are no physical office spaces to provide this. An effective way to define a team boundary is to use the team API from Chapter 2 of this workbook.

Find teams that are willing to explore the use of a team API to help them work better together as a team. Suggest that teams work together to explore and refine an approach that works for documenting and broadcasting the team API of each team: a wiki, an internal website, a code repository, an online whiteboard tool, or something similar.

After a suitable, workable approach has been established, hold a series of showcase sessions where teams that have started using a team API can share their experiences with other teams. Explain why the team API is being introduced and how it can help to increase the clarity of purpose for teams.

Don't forget to include details of current and expected team interaction modes within the team API showcase sessions (see Chapter 4 in this workbook). The ways in which teams interact and the purpose of the interaction is a key indicator of organizational effectiveness. Encouraging teams to think about the team interactions will help them to become more effective within the organization as a whole.

Devise and Share an Execution Plan

Meet with other people in the organization to discuss how to try some of the ideas and patterns in this workbook. Begin by identifying which techniques could be most useful immediately and start with those.

Revisit this workbook on a regular basis to see what else you could or should be doing. What have you learned from previous techniques? Can you improve how some techniques are being used?

If you need to increase shared understanding across multiple teams, consider some more formal or structured approaches, such as lunchtime chats, nonwork afternoons, internal tech conferences, etc. These sessions can have a substantial impact if the talks are prepared in advance and the speakers are confident in the delivery of the details. *Internal Tech Conferences* by Victoria Morgan-Smith and Matthew Skelton provides additional tips and tricks for a successful internal event.

List of Resources

"Getting Started" and "Team Topologies in a Nutshell" infographics
teamtopologies.com/infographics.

Engineering Experience Feedback Survey: ITRev.io/EngExpFeedback.

Online Space Assessment Template
GitHub.com/TeamTopologies/Online-Space-Assessment.

Team API template
GitHub.com/TeamTopologies/Team-API-Template.

Team Cognitive Load Assessment
GitHub.com/TeamTopologies/Team-Cognitive-Load-Assessment.

Team Dependencies tracker
GitHub.com/TeamTopologies/Team-Dependencies-Tracking.

Team Interaction Diagram Shapes
Shapes.TeamTopologies.com.

Thinnest Viable Platform Template
GitHub.com/TeamTopologies/Thin-Platform-Template.

Trust Boundaries Template
GitHub.com/TeamTopologies/Trust-Boundaries-Template.

Notes

Chapter 1

1. Julia Rozovsky, "The Five Keys to a Successful Google Team," *ReWork*, November 17, 2015. https://rework.withgoogle.com/blog/five-keys-to-a -successful-google-team/.
2. Rozovsky, "The Five Keys."
3. Dominica DeGrandis, "How to Defrag Your DevOps Value Stream," *TechBeacon*, accessed January 2022, https://techbeacon.com/app-dev-testing/how-defrag-your-devops-value-stream.
4. Meaghan Lewis, "Remote Testing Teams: How to Overcome Key Challenges," *TechBeacon*, accessed November 11, 2021, https://techbeacon.com /app-dev-testing/remote-testing-teams-how-overcome-key-challenges.

Chapter 2

1. Jon Patterson, communication with the authors, November 2021.
2. Henrik Kniberg and Anders Ivarsson, *Scaling Agile @ Spotify with Tribes, Squads, Chapters & Guilds*, October 2021, https://blog.crisp.se/wp -content/uploads/2012/11/SpotifyScaling.pdf.
3. Longqi Yang et. al., "The Effects of Remote Work on Collaboration among Information Workers," *Nature Human Behaviour*, September 9, 2021, https://www.nature.com/articles/s41562-021-01196-4.
4. Yang et. al., "The Effects of Remote Work."
5. David Heath (@dgheath21), "Are you aware of any organisations who have taken steps to pro-actively counteract these tendencies? I've experimented with running open cross-organisation speed-networking sessions (3x5 minute pairwise conversations using video breakout rooms)." Twitter, September 10, 2021, https://twitter.com/dgheath21/status/ 1436338206186872835.

6. Emily Webber, *Building Successful Communities of Practice: Discover How Connecting People Makes Better Organisations*, Blurb, 2016, 11.

7. Sarah Wells, "Engine Room 2020: Going Virtual," Financial Times, December 3, 2020. https://medium.com/ft-product-technology/engine-room-2020 -going-virtual-7d4f77bc2969.

Chapter 3

1. Emily Webber, "Dunbar's Numbers and Communities of Practice—Q and A with Emily Webber," TeamTopologies.com, June 1, 2020, https://team topologies.com/news/dunbars-numbers-and-communities-of-practice-q -and-a-with-emily-webber.

2. Ben Ford, "Organisational Size Phase Transition Points," *Commando Development*, (February 9, 2020). https://commando.dev/writing/social- inflection-points/.

3. Individual communication with the authors.

4. Karl Stoney (@karlstoney), "1/3 We did a simple but cool thing recently, our platform now maps your service metadata (a file in your repo) to a dynamically created @SlackHQ group as part of your deployments. Super useful for pulling in maintainers to conversations/incidents etc rather than looking them up." Twitter, August 16, 2021, https://twitter.com/karlstoney/ status/1427351171853918217?s=20.

Chapter 4

1. Ethan Bernstein, Jesse Shore, and David Lazer, "How Intermittent Breaks in Interaction Improve Collective Intelligence," *Proceedings of the National Academy of Sciences of the United States of America* 115, no. 35 (August 28, 2018), https://www.pnas.org/content/115/35/8734.

2. "Equal Experts / slack-guide," GitHub repository. https://github.com /EqualExperts/slack-guide.

3. Tom Clark, "ITV's Common Platform v2 Better, Faster, Cheaper, Happier," presentation at DevOps Enterprise Summit London 2019. https://videos .itrevolution.com/watch/505445404/.

4. Clark, "ITV's Common Platform."

5. Clark, "ITV's Common Platform."

Chapter 5

1 Justin Kitagawa, "Platforms at Twilio: Unlocking Developer Effectiveness," presentation at QCon 2018, https://www.infoq.com/presentations/twilio -devops/.

About the Authors

Matthew Skelton is coauthor of *Team Topologies: Organizing Business and Technology Teams for Fast Flow*. Recognized by TechBeacon in 2018, 2019, and 2020 as one of the top one hundred people to follow in DevOps, Matthew curates the well-known DevOps team topologies patterns at DevOpsTopologies.com. He is head of consulting at Conflux and specializes in continuous delivery, operability, and organization dynamics for modern software systems.

Manuel Pais is coauthor of *Team Topologies: Organizing Business and Technology Teams for Fast Flow*. Recognized by TechBeacon as a DevOps thought leader, Manuel is an independent IT organizational consultant and trainer, focused on team interactions, delivery practices, and accelerating flow. Manuel is also a LinkedIn instructor on continuous delivery.

About Team Topologies

In *Team Topologies*, IT consultants Matthew Skelton and Manuel Pais share secrets of successful team patterns and interactions to help IT organizations choose and evolve the right team patterns to ensure success, making sure to keep the software healthy and to optimize for value streams.

Team Topologies will help readers discover:

- team patterns used by successful organizations
- common team patterns to avoid with modern software systems
- when and why to use different team patterns
- how to evolve teams effectively
- how to split software and align to teams